Letter From an Heritor to his Fellows, the Landed Interest of Scotland, to Meet in Delegation at Edinburgh, on Monday, July 2. 1792

LETTER

TO

DELEGATES,

30th June 1792.

———

NISI DIGNUS VINDICE.

———

LETTER

FROM

AN HERITOR

TO

HIS FELLOWS,

THE

LANDED INTEREST

OF

SCOTLAND,

TO MEET IN

DELEGATION AT EDINBURGH,

ON MONDAY, JULY 2. 1792.

Si bonum quicquid accipite, rejicite quod catvium.

EDINBURGH:

PRINTED FOR THE AUTHOR

M,DCC,XCII.

ADVERTISEMENT.

THE Editor throws out to his Country the following thoughts, on a subject of no small importance, viz. The settling the Right of Franchise or voting in County Elections upon a more enlarged and permanent footing than at present, yet consistent with the established Constitution of this part of the united kingdom. Not afraid to handle a subject involving in part the great question of Parliamentary Reform, in so far as seems safe, but protesting that he has not been the mover. It was started by gentlemen whose names he does not know, with, he is persuaded, pure intentions, and convinced, that had the justly-condemned Association been first formed, their patriotism would have checked their zeal for the present; and pointing out the danger of doing harm where good was intended, would have suggested, that it is better to submit to known inconvenience, than lose a good improvement by untimely attempt.

T O,

SIR ALEXANDER RAMSAY

OF BALMAIN, Bart,

PRESES OF THE LATE MEETING OF GENTLEMEN OF PROPERTY IN
SCOTLAND, AT EDINBURGH, APRIL 1792.

SIR,

TO none with fo much propriety as to you can the following Letter be infcribed, the Gentlemen with whom you
met at Edinburgh on the 24th of April laft, having placed you
in the chair of a meeting, refpectable, as I am informed, for
independent property, and principles the moft conftitutional,
yet diftinguifhed by no party-attachment, but affembled by
that active zeal for the real good of their country, which, called forth on urgent occafions, moving with fteady pace, equally
firm and circumfpect, proves a beneficent ftream, enriching as
it flows, not a torrent overwhelming in its courfe, removing ob-
ftruction by violence, and bringing deftruction on the land it
ought to benefit.

B   That

That the approaching meeting of Delegates of the Heritors of the Counties of Scotland may prove the beneficent ſtream, is my earneſt prayer, for the good of our country, in which I have ſome intereſt, my love for which, and my attachment to its excellent conſtitution, induce me to addreſs this letter to you, to the Delegates, to my Country, and to the Public at large, and which is a hazardous ſtep for the firſt time to appear in print.

This Letter comes anonymous, not that I am aſhamed of the name I bear, but becauſe a good or bad plan ſhould be received or rejected on its own merits, not on the ſuppoſed merit or de-merit of

The AUTHOR.

L E T T E R

T O

The COURT of DELEGATES to meet at Edinburgh, July 2. 1792.

Gentlemen,

DELEGATED by the heritors of Scotland to confider of the
prefent ftate of their reprefentation in Parliament, and of
the beft means of remedying the acknowledged defects in it, fo
far as relates to the Right of Voting at the Election of the Reprefentatives for Shires in Scotland, commonly ftyled County
Members, admit an addrefs from an Heritor of no incon-
fiderable property;—of what extent, is immaterial to the prefent queftion,—of what clafs or name, is equally unimpor-
tant. The magnitude of the object of difcuffion, no lefs than
the confirming, ftrengthening, and rendering more durable the
Conftitution of this country, which we have fo recently in county-meetings refolved anew to maintain againft all infidious and
feditious attempts tending to undermine or deftroy, fealed
with our names, and carried in our addreffes to the foot of the
Throne; thus moft folemnly ratifying, fwearing to maintain
for ourfelves, and hand down to pofterity unimpaired, that excellent conftitution eftablifhed by our anceftors at the glorious
Revolution in 1688, bought by and fealed with their blood, at
at the expence of a race of Kings who had worn the Crown of

this

this kingdom 318 years, a period long enough to have eftablifhed hereditary right, if fuch could exift in a free kingdom without the confent and approbation of the people but they had rendered their own expulfion neceffary, for *falus populi fuprema lex eft*. This I hold to be the firft Revolution principle, and the only one on which it can be juftified. A nation is bound by fealty to its Sovereign, a people muft fuffer long, muft bear much, before they think of changing, which can be warranted by neceffity alone, and the fupreme law of public fafety. This warrant James VII. * gave our forefathers, and this they executed againft him and his defcendants, by excluding him from returning, and his fon (who had been acknowledged as fuch in England) from the fucceffion, and by chufing others to occupy the throne declared vacant. Whether James abdicated, whether he renounced for himfelf and his fons, whether he was driven, expelled, or vacated the Crown, is immaterial. The doctrine laid down then, and maintained ever fince by the nation, is, " That " a King on whom the Crown has devolved by inheritance, hold- " ing it by the law of the land, can, by violating that law, for- " feit the Crown for himfelf and defcendants. then and then " only it reverts to the people, to difpofe of as they judge " moft for the public good, taking the next in fucceffion quali- " fied to wear it, with power to annex to it what conditions and " limitations they fee expedient for the public fafety." This they did, and this we maintain they did of right every time we take the oaths of fidelity, allegiance, and abjuration. The record of Parliament, the ftatute-book, preferves in it acts of fecurity and fucceffion. In thofe very acts which placed that Crown, fo happily for this nation, on the heads of the Brunfwick line, which had, fo unhappily for them, fallen from the heads of the Houfe of Steuart, there it is written, there it may be feen,

---

* I fpeak as a Scotfman.

how the transfer was made, and by what unpredictable steps Providence brought about the wonderful change· While we admire let us also bless the invisible hand which thus strengthened and confirmed the rights and privileges of these nations, and secured to us our happy constitution, the blessing of these, the admiration and envy of surrounding nations, the ultimate inheritance, I most devoutly hope, of all the world; for it is no bad wish surely to others, to pray that they may be as blessed as we, with a constitution conferring security and happiness exceeding example, and surpassing all human wisdom to contrive.

This love of and zeal in support of our happy constitution, does not blind me so far as to make me think it above all improvement, or to preclude all amendment or reform. There is no absolute perfection upon earth. It is presumption to say that we may not approach nearer to it. But there is no hazard in warning ourselves to beware of innovations, to move cautiously in reform, and even to amend with discretion, after the most mature deliberation. In some cases, there is a danger in experiment: but there is as much weakness, on the other hand, in rejecting all amendment, and every reform. Of these we have had multiplied instances, and felt many good effects: they have operated improvement, they have led towards perfection; but as for innovation, destruction lies in the way; let us beware, let us avoid it.

After thus premising, what I have to offer on the subject of Freehold Qualifications may appear bold, and tending to hazardous innovation. In that I should possibly agree, were the idea new, were it now first broached, and had it not been actually proposed by the Freeholders of some counties at their Michaelmas head-courts.

Let it however be remembered, that the qualification of Free-

C

holders

holders is but, *A legal declaration of the right of franchise*, and not an alteration of the conftitution, inconfiftent with which, it is contended, no alteration ought, or can be made agreeable to public fafety; yet without endangering either, and poffibly with advantage to both, fome change may probably be effected. This appears, from their refolutions, and from your appointment, Gentlemen, to be the opinion of the Landholders of moft of the counties in Scotland.

Such fhires as have not fent Delegates feem to have confidered the importance of this fubject too lightly, or (what I am averfe to fuppofe) reft contented with the generally acknowledged ill ftate of this thing, indolently fubmitting to grievances felt by all, and which may with perfect fafety be removed, was the public mind fufficiently well informed to fix upon a prudent and practicable plan of reform, neither inconfiftent with, nor adverfe to our juftly-efteemed conftitution.

It is not my bufinefs to guefs at, or animadvert on the views of particular claffes of men, or of individuals; they may have their views it is enough for me that the public is concerned, and that that public is my country. If the plan produced does not correfpond with their good, reject; if it promifes benefit, why not adopt it?

* A moft illuftrious authority lately, in a folemn proteftation in the higheft affembly in the nation, laid down this truly conftitutional principle, " *That all reform not fanctioned by the people* " *is wrong.*" It follows, we may fairly infer, " That reforms " may with fafety be made, when fo fanctioned." And the late royal proclamation, confidered as a minifterial appeal to the people, with the confequent addreffes, confirm and fanction the inference.

* His Royal Highnefs the Prince of Wales.

We

We come now to the point. You Gentlemen Delegates are deputed by the heritors of Scotland * to meet at Edinburgh, to form a court to confider the laws of election for fhires ; And no more! What would be the ufe of that ? You may confider thofe laws more at leifure, and ftudy *Wight on Elections* more coolly, at your own homes in the country; (for I prefume you all have homes in thofe counties whence you come), than in the metropolis in the month of July, when our legiflature has wifely thought it better to fend our lawyers and judges into the country for refefhment, than to detain them later in the inner-houfe ; when our Chief Magiftrate finds it time to fend his counfellors into the country ; and when none chufe to do bufinefs in towns who can get out of them.

Why then fhould you be fent to ftudy our election-code in town in the heats, which too often excites ferment in autumn, but that the collective judgement of the wifeft men † of this kingdom may be obtained on a fubject fo extenfively important ; and that you may, from fuch collection of judgement and full information, form fome plan to be laid before your conftituents in your report, which you can propofe to them as practicable, fafe, and ufeful, upon which they may form the heads of a bill for a new law, and inftruct their members to bring into Parliament, it generally approved of.

I fhall prefume to hint, that the form of refolutions, to be adopted, altered, or rejected by the county-meetings, may be pre-

---

* It is not now debated, whether Peers may be received as Delegates or not, or how far they are concerned in the county-reprefentation. But if any are fent, it fhews the fenfe of thofe counties who delegated them.

† It is prefumed, the wifeft would be delegated from each fhire.

ferable

ferable to heads drawn up, who may then renew their commif-
fion of delegates, with powers to prepare the heads of a bill di-
gefted on thofe principles moft generally approven, for to wait
till an unanimous approbation can be obtained, would be as abfurd as to expect a plan to be formed without concert, or carried into effect without agreement It would defeat every good
purpofe, and ferve the end of thofe only who find, or delufively
think they fee, their intereft in confufion.

You may perceive, Gentlemen, I do not write as a lawyer;
a character to which I have no pretenfions, I do not affume
it. that of a plain honeft countryman is all I afpire to; a fair
ambit on furely to every man in a free ftate neither pretending to
be a man of letters, or profound politician, they are often fwerved
by prejudices of education and practice. much lefs a modern
philofopher; they overturn every thing old, to fet up new fyftems
equally abfurd and inapplicable, (to our fituation at leaft), upon
new-fangled and unintelligible doctrines, fpecioufly mifleading
the unwary and well-intentioned with defcriptions of unat-
tainable perfection. It is enough for me to have a little confidered this fubject on which I venture to addrefs you; and that
my fellows, the landed intereft of Scotland, are deeply interefted
in it; happy if any propofition from fo weak a pen can tend to
utility, and amply rewarded fhould it produce fome falutary
effect.

Reform.
If no reform is needed, then the only ufe of the Delegation is
to exprefs it as their opinion. But that fome reform is become
neceffary, from the degenerate ftate of things, and that the conftitution of Scotland has in this refpect fo * far *flid from its bafis,*

* Speech of Chancellor Thurlow upon a Scotch election caufe, 1789.

as

as to need a parliamentary repair, your nomination fhews it to be the general fenfe, and that fome propofition towards its repair is expected from you · Therefore I may prophetically foretel, that fhould you feparate without forming fome plan, difappointment will follow; but fhould that plan be made on a contracted fcale, difapprobation will enfue. Thefe are not times to narrow privileges. Any fuch attempt muft produce difcontent, whence would flow murmur, commotion, and eventually fubverfion.

Had no fuch queftion been ftarted, perhaps I might have been led, from fome late events, to think it fhould not now be agitated, but the complaint is not new in Scotland, it is of long ftanding; the inconvenience is not fmall, the grievance has been loudly complained of. Thefe, and the circumftances of the times, with the reafonablenefs of the thing itfelf, in a country advancing faft in liberality, improvements, and cultivation, by induftry to wealth, indicate that no narrowing fyftem will be well received; but that we muft, inftead of retrograding, look forward, and provide for farther improvement, by approaching nearer to the fyftem of our more advanced neighbours the Englifh, with whom we are now indiffolubly connected.

The only way, then, to get rid of the inconveniences felt and complained of — to repair and ftrengthen the Conftitution, and to fet it up again erect, firm, and permanent upon its bafis, feems to be, *By lowering the qualification, and attaching the right of franchife to the actual poffeffion of the property, fuch proprietor being the vaffal of the Crown.*

Thus the Conftitution will be preferved and ftrengthened, while the grievance will be removed, as no *parchment* Freeholder could then claim to vote at Elections for our fhires · Neither could the fubject-fuperior, by fplitting his valuation, extend an

D   undue

undue influence over the poffeffors of the property of the county, or place on the roll a phalanx of confidential voters, frequently unconnected with the county, and always accufed, often falfely indeed, of being devoted to the will, and obedient to the mandates of their creator . — A practice fufficiently known in Scotland to have excited much difcord, though poffibly little experienced to the fouth of the Tweed.

To fee how fuch a meafure may be adopted without injury to, nay, with the fafety and improvement of the Conftitution, let us confider what the Conftitution is in this particular. I take it to be, " *That the vaffal of the Crown, infeft in lands to a cer-* " *tain extent, fhall have right to vote.*" Now poffeffion is prefumed to follow infeftment , the eye of the law hath no other contemplation , and as vaffalage is a feudal tenure, it fees no other but the immediate vaffal of the Crown This is termed *freehold,* but admits of fub-vaffalage , fo that the holding of the Crown, with the infeftment, conftitute the right of voting — not the *actual poffeffion of the eftate.* *Hinc origo mali,* becaufe I can buy an eftate holding of the Crown , I can feu it out at full value blanch, and I, not the poffeffor, am the voter. — This is good in law, though the purpofe is direct.

Again, I can purchafe a fuperiority of a blanch holding, and I, not the proprietor of the eftate, am the voter.

This is termed a freehold, and rightly; becaufe holding of the Crown is holding of no body, for the Crown has no reftraining authority over the holder.

It does not appear, then, that adding an eftate in real poffeffion to the holding can weaken that independence effential to conftitute a freehold. I think it is ftrengthening it.

Why

Conftitution of Freehold Qualification

Why then lower the qualifications ?—Becaufe the times and the progrefs of things require it.—An eftate of L. 100 of valued rent is now often of more value than one of L. 400 was one hundred years ago; and the proprietor generally a man of greater refpectability, and no lefs ancient defcent.—But be it remembered, that poffeffion, not defcent, is the requifite—elfe where are your parchment Barons ?—In this particular our an-ceftors, attached as they were to family brieves, never fpoke of defcent, but of poffeffion.—Have we narrowed that doctrine ?

If, then, this can be adopted with fafety, let us fee the expe-diency. But firft look how the law ftands. Go back to James I. parliament 3. act 52. *Item*, it is ordained, &c.

" That all Prelates, Erles, Baronnes, and *Freehalders of the*
" *King*, be halden to compeir in perfon, and not be a procura-
" tour; but gif (unlefs) the procuratour alleage there and prove
" a lauchful caufe of their abfence." 1425 Ja I parl 3. act 52

Here appears to have been a practice of voting by proxy, as the perfonal attendance on the King's parliament was often in-convenient; which practice by that ftatute is reftrained, and per-fonal prefence infifted on.

This being found fo burdenfome as not to be exigible by law, or compellable by force, it was ordained by ftatute James I. parl. 3. act 101.

" That fmall baronnes and free tenentes need not cum to par-
" liaments, but are to fend two reprefentatives from each fhe-
" riffdome, called Commiffaries or Commiffioners of Shires." Perfonal attendance 1427 Ja I. parl 3. act 101

So here we have that reprefentation eftablifhed which obtains

to

to this day, as an indulgence to the King's leſſer vaſſals, the great ones (or greater Barons) being bound in perſonal preſence on the King's ſummons.

1457 Ja. II parl 13 act 75

A diſtinction is drawn by exempting freeholders under L. 20 Scots.

1503 Ja. IV parl. 3 act 78

That all freeholders under 100 merks of extent *ſend their procurators to parliament*

1587 Ja. VI parl. 11 act 114

" Act of James I. ratified.—Precepts from the King for chu-
" ſing commiſſioners of ſhires.—Men of gude rent, indwellers
" of the ſhire, *and* that *all* freeholders of the King, under the
" degree of Prelates and Lords of Parliament, to be preſent at
" the chooſing of the ſaid commiſſioners; and *nane* to have *voit*

Commiſſioners of ſhires and their qualifications.

Electors.

Their qualification, a Forty ſhilling land holden of the King

" in their election bot *ſik* as hes fourtie-ſhilling land in *free te-*
" *nendry halden of the King*, and hes their actual dwelling and
" reſidence within the ſame ſhire. Theſe commiſſioners to be
" elected annually at the Michaelmas head-court."

1597 Ja. VI parl. 15 act 276

" Baronnes ſuld ſend to parliament commiſſioners with ſuffi-
" cient commiſſions."

Thus far the way is clear, the line of repreſentation is diſtinct from James the I. to VI. " That the real freeholders, vaſſals of " the Crown, poſſeſſing their own lands, ſhall vote upon the e- " ſtates they hold." And if any deviation was afterwards made, they, in ſo far, departed from the original principle of the Con- ſtitution, viz. *The repreſentation of the Eſtates, as well as of the perſons of the Barons*, a principle never to be loſt ſight of, and to which, if it has by law or practice been deviated from, a new law ſhould recall the practice, ſhort of which, nothing effectual- ly ſalutary can be done. Palliatives would be tampering with

the

the Conftitution, and by weakening, endanger it. Why then fhould we not repair it? why leave to others, at fo imminent a rifk, to do that which, by applying the remedy ourfelves, we may do, and leave it to our fucceffors in a more improved ftate than we received it?

The right of voting extended to " all heritors, liferenters, and " wadfetters, holding of the King or Prince, of ten chalders, or " L. 1000 Scots of valued rent." 1661 Cha II. parl. 1, act 35.

It is to be obferved, that by this law the right of franchife was communicated to many who did not before enjoy it, particularly to fuch as formerly held of bifhops or abbots. But in twenty years after a farther extenfion was made, at which it has continued to this day; for thereby it is ftatuted and ordained, " That 1681 Cha. II parl. 3. act 21. " *none* fhall have vote in the election of commiffioners of fhires, " but thofe who at that time fhall be publicly infeft in *property* " or *fuperiority*, and in poffeffion of a forty-fhilling land of old " extent, holden of the King or Prince, diftinct from the feu- " duties in feu lands; or where the faid old extent appears not, " fhall be infeft in lands liable in public burden for his Majefty's " fupplies, for *four hundred pounds of valued rent*, whether kirk- " lands now holden of the king, or other lands holding feu, " ward, or blanch of his Majefty, as King or Prince of Scotland."

Proper wadfetters, heirs apparent in poffeffion, liferenters, hufbands in right of their wives, and fiars, have right to vote.

Not taking the teft a fufficient objection.

Here the principle of poffeffion is departed from; the fuperior is allowed to vote, and may be a wadfetter, liferenter, or fiar

E

of

of a forty-shilling land, or L. 400 Scots of valued rent, holden blanch. Can there be a more aerial property, *no residence, no domicil, no property* ! A mere possession of *nothing*, acquired without *purchase*, except the fees of the seal of the charter, completed by form of infeftment, constitutes a franchise, and legally creates a *parchment baron*. What absurdity ! That persons having no actual property, not contributing to the expences of the State, shall have power to bind those who do. The reign in which this was done, in which the abominable test was enacted in Scotland, (afterwards happily repealed), and subsequent to it, sufficiently demonstrates the arbitrary design to disqualify *all non-conforming Freeholders*, to the plan of cramming Episcopacy down the throats of the Scotch. But that stubborn people, as history informs us, attached to their rights, resisted, and would not be dragooned into forms they detested.

At the glorious Revolution in 1688, they established their rights, civil and religious, but, satisfied with the repeal of the Test, and not perceiving the extent of the evil of the act 1681, left it in force.

At the Union in 1707, they confirmed those rights, but neglected so favourable an opportunity to replace the Constitution, which had thus *slid from its basis*, on its ancient solid foundation of property, from whence it has been farther sliding ever since ; and considering the ineffectual attempts made, and so frequently repeated, to restrain the evil consequences which have produced the grievances now complained of, of which we have had but too much experience

1713 Anne 11.
1727 Geo II 1
1728 Geo II 2
1735 Geo II 7
1742 Geo. II 16

It seems evident, that no other method is left to restore the Constitution, but to place it again upon the original basis of *property held of the Crown*; and in so doing, not to narrow, but extend

tend the privilege, by lowering the qualification *below Four hundred pounds Scots of valued-rent*; how far is matter of deliberation and discretion.

I think I have now shown, that in so doing, the Constitution will neither be departed from nor impaired, but restored, strengthened, and replaced where it stood at first in ancient times, and where alone it ought to stand in all future ages.

That the old acts were constitutional has been shown. That the act 1681 was violently aristocratical, and ought not to be reverted to, is evident. For, however aristocratical, and severely felt so, the government of Scotland formerly was; yet in these last 100 years, that aristocracy, under which a free and commercial nation cannot thrive, has been so wisely limited, so well tempered and intermixed with democratical ingredients, that they are nearly as well blended now in Scotland as they have long been in England, and sufficiently for the public good; for we have a mixed government suited to our interest and habits, and happily interwoven, so as to form a whole, more perfect than in other countries. Thence, under the blessings of Divine Providence, flows that happiness we feel, and exult in enjoying. Let us then hold it sacred, let us not depart from it, let us not put to our hands to pull our own good house down; but join in its support.

Were this plan of *conjoining the actual property with the superiority* in the person of the freeholder to be adopted, who could suffer?

1*st*, The subject superior fiar.—Let him hold what he has, let him transmit it to his heirs, but let him not transfer it to another except to his vassal the possessor.

2*d*, The subject superior liferenter.—Life is short, let him hold it for life.

3*d*, The subject husband in right of his wife superior.—So slippery a right seems scarce worth holding; let him keep it who can.

4*th*, The subject superior proper wadsetter.—This slender holding is hardly perceptible; where it exists let it remain, but suffer it not to be transferred or renewed.

5*th*, And perhaps the greatest injury is the privation of the possessed power in proprietors of considerable estates, and the great families of the kingdom of Scotland.

Here I confess difficulty occurs, but not unsurmountable, where the greater good of the country is at stake.

The great men of the kingdom, like the officers of a regiment, are commissioned for its good order and support. They are always to sacrifice their private interests, nay their lives, to the good of the State. They are to set example, as they are to watch over it. The Nobility of Scotland have ever been distinguished for this patriotic loyalty. And no doubt can be entertained, but they of our day will prove themselves worthy of their ancient honours, by cheerfully complying with the good of their country. What reward have they? The reward of all honest men, the praise of their country, and the consciousness of having done it service. That honest influence, which follows property, family, and personal worth, in public esteem. What other can they desire? Perhaps you may think it just to add, the eligibility to Parliament of the eldest sons of Peers, a privilege of which they seem to have been deprived in Scotland, by the not ill-founded jealousy of the Commons.

6*th*, And

6th, And leaft, The diminution of the individual importance of the leffer Barons. This will be found to be in fo fmall a degree, as not to be fenfibly felt by gentlemen of property, who, relieved by this new operation from that oppreffion they have for many years laboured under, will, by the admiffion of their fmaller neighbours and friends to the roll of freeholders, clear it of thofe they relu&antly admit and wifh to exclude; get rid of the grievance; and gaining on one hand more than they lofe on the other, will find their account in it, as fplitting of valuation will thereby be abolifhed in Scotland.

Si quid novifti rectius iftis, candidus imperti, fi non, his utere

With,

Gentlemen,

Your moft Obedient,

Devoted, and Faithful Servant,

AN HERITOR.

30th June,
1 7 9 2.